Crochet for Kids

How to Teach a Child Crochet: 8 Crochet for Kids

Table of Content

Introduction

Some of the best memories are made of the simplest things in life. Since we're all crocheters at heart what better gift to give others than to teach crochet? With How to Teach a Child to Crochet 8 Crochet Projects for Kids, we will discuss tips on starting with kids and crochet.

Crochet lessons can start when children are at young ages but it depends on the individual. Learning to teach kids to crochet is rewarding and provides them with a lifelong skill that they can work on improving every year.

1. How to Crochet a Chain Stitch

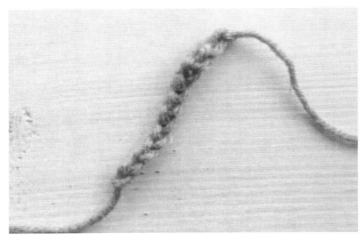

Calling all crochet beginners to come check out this How to Crochet a Chain Stitch tutorial. This is a great crochet tutorial to show you a very important skill when crocheting.

If you are just starting off learning how to crochet and you aren't quite sure how to make a slip knot or a chain, this tutorial is the perfect way for you to see how it's done.

Materials List
- Crochet hook
- Yarn

How to Make a Chain Stitch:
- Make a slip knot.

- Do this by placing the end of the yarn across your hand, and then wrap the working yarn around two of your fingers, making a little fish shape.
- Then take your hook, go through the big loop (the fish face) and grab the far piece of yarn (fish tail) and pull it back through the big loop (the fish face).
- Tighten that from there so that you have your loop.
- Tip: You will know if your slip knot is correct if it can be pulled larger and smaller freely.

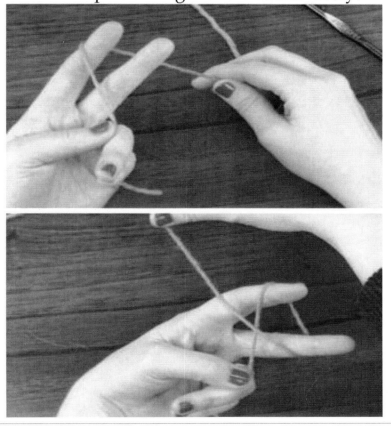

- Put your working yarn to the left and the tail to the right.
- Hold the working yarn the way it is comfortable to you, like running it between your fingers as shown.
- To chain, wrap the working yarn around your hook from behind, and pull it through your loop.

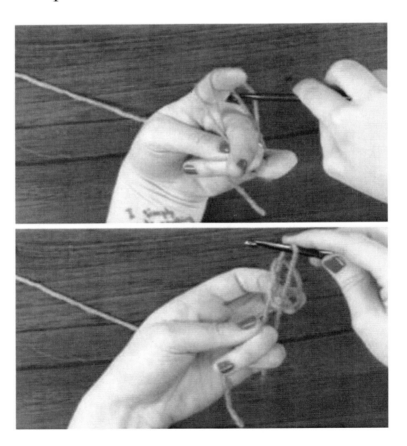

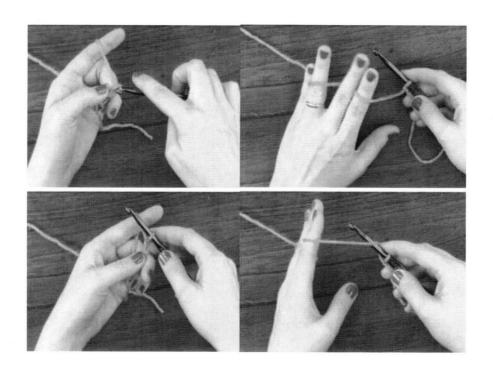

- Repeat that process until you have added as many chains as you need.
- Tip: Do not work your chain too tightly. Then it will be really hard to work in those stitches through out the next row.

- "To know how many stitches you have chained, look for each V of the teardrop. The back of a chain stitch has bumps, do not count that side." - Heidi Gustad

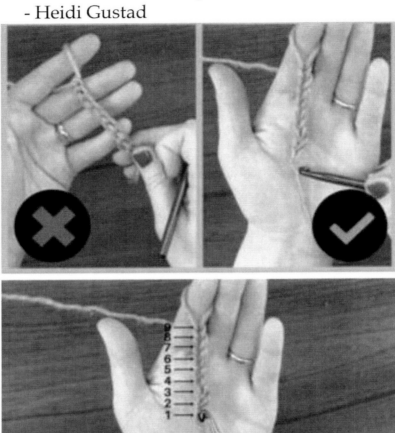

2. Rainbow Friendship Bracelet.

"This Rainbow Friendship Bracelet can be crocheted, from start to finish, in less than 10 minutes. This bracelet can be easily customized to different sizes as it is worked lengthwise. You can simply tie the ends together to be worn on a friend's wrist, or you can stitch the two ends together and slide it over your own hand to wear. Friendship bracelets are fantastic beginner level crochet projects, as you can practice your stitches and have a gift to show for your time and effort."

Supplies:
- Aunt Lydia's Classic 10 Crochet Thread

- mm (B) Crochet Hook

Abbreviations Used: R – row, sc – single crochet, ch – chain, st – stitch, sts – stitches

Bracelet Lengths: *Please note these are approximate lengths and the actual wrist size will vary from person to person. If you do not have an exact wrist size for the person you wish to give the bracelet to, the easiest way to make one to fit would be to finish off leaving a tail for tying the bracelet in place. Try it on the wrist and if it is too large then remove the last few rows until it fits and then tie it on!*

Children:
- 2-3 years: 5.0"
- 4-5 years: 5.5"
- 6-7 years: 6.0"
- 8-9 years: 6.25"
- 10-11 years: 6.5"
- 12-13 years: 7"

Women:
- Small 7.5"
- Medium 8 "
- Large 8.5"

Rainbow Friendship Bracelet Pattern
R1: ch 3, begin in the 2nd ch from the hook and work 1 sc in each of the next 2 sts, ch 1, turn (2)

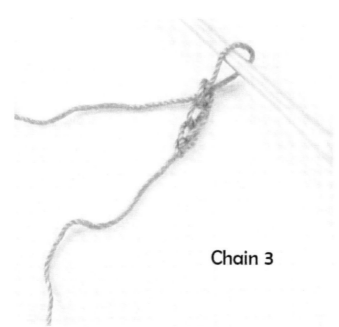

Chain 3

- R2: work 1 sc in each of the 2 sts, ch 1, turn (2)

2 sts, ch 1, turn

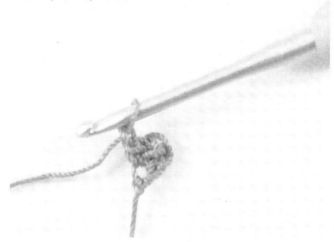

- R3: work 1 sc in each of the 2 sts, ch 1, turn (2)
- R4 – End: repeat R3 until your bracelet measures the length you want (see size options listed above if needed)

Work 1 sc in each of the 2 sts, ch 1, turn

Super simple right? If you are teaching someone to crochet this would be a good starting project – it allows them to practise some very basic stitches and in the end they have something to show for their work. Learning something new is always much more fun when you can walk away with a finished item.

3. Five Pental Flower.

Crocheting a flower is easier than you might think, so follow along with this video and let us teach you how to work up your very own crochet flowers! Our tutorial, How to Crochet a Five Petal Flower for Beginners, is a great how-to to start with.

Materials List
- Crochet hook of choice
- Yarn of choice
- Scissors

How to Make Easy Crochet Flowers:

- Ch 4.

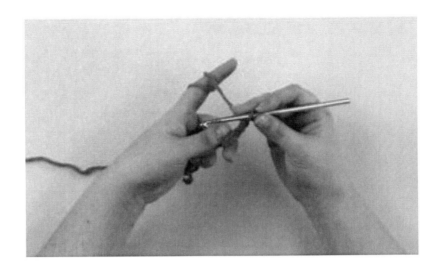

- Sl st into the first stitch of the chain. This creates a little ring.
-

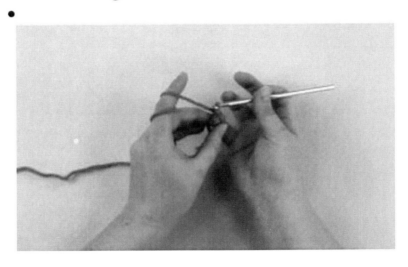

- Rnd 1: 2sc in next chain. Ch 1, sc. Repeat all the way around.

Tip: If you crochet over the tail as you go, you won't have to weave in as much.

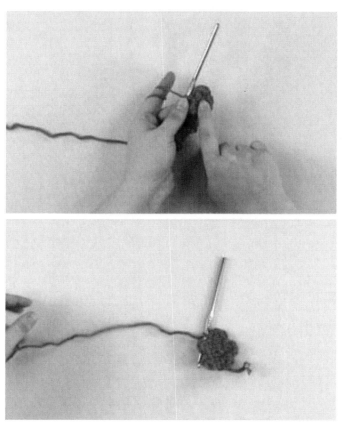

- Finish off and weave in any ends.

Tip: If you leave a long tail, it can be used to attach the flower later. Keep this in mind!

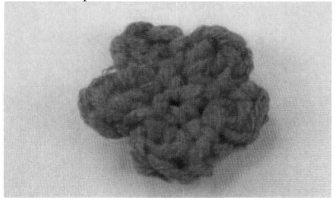

4. Cute Washcloth for Bath.

This is an super easy washcloth of bath scrubbie, perfect for bath time!! Beginner level and perfect for gifts. As an extra, there is also a round scrubbie tutorial!

Crochet Hook: F/5 or 3.75 mm hook

Yarn Weight(4): Medium Weight/Worsted Weight and Aran (16-20 stitches to 4 inches)

Crochet Gauge: Gauge is not critical.

Materials List
- Yarn

- Hook
- Optional Yarn Needle
- Ribbon to tie. Optional

Instructions

Washcloth scrubbie:

- Rnd 1:Ch 15-20 . Double Crochet in the row across.
- Rnd 2-10:Ch 3, double crochet in the row across. Fasten off.

To gift or decorate for display,roll and tie a ribbon on the roll. Gift or Enjoy yourself.

Round Scrubbie:

- Rnd 1: Chain 4. Slip Stitch in 1st chain.Double crochet 14 times in circle.sl st to join in first chain.
- Rnd 2: Chain 3.DC twice in first chain, 1 dc in second chain. Repeat till end of round.sl st to join. Then fasten off.

5. Quick Crochet Butterfly Pattern.

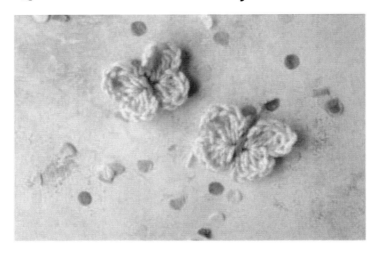

This Quick Crochet Butterfly Pattern is by and large the easiest way you will ever see to crochet a butterfly. As you make this crochet butterfly you are only working in one round, so after you complete your chain you are one and done. Plus, this is a great crochet pattern to work on if you need to use up some scrap yarn.

Crochet Hook: H/8 or 5 mm hook

Yarn Weight(4): Medium Weight/Worsted Weight and Aran (16-20 stitches to 4 inches)

Finished Size: 1.5-2 inches

Materials List

- Yarn: 1 main color and scrap of another color. | Featured in this Video: Premier Deborah Norville Everyday Collection
- Crochet hook

How to Crochet a Butterfly Instructions

Note: The butterfly is made in 1 round, finished with tying a piece of yarn around middle.

- Ch 4, sl st to the first chain to join.

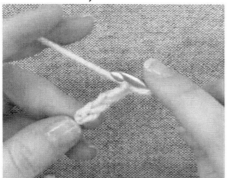 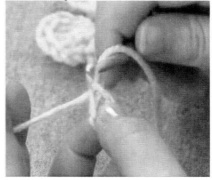

- Rnd 1: Ch 2, dc 3, ch 1, sl st to the ring. Ch 3, tr 3, ch 2, sl st to the ring, ch 2, tr 3, ch 3, sl st to the ring, ch 2, dc 3, ch 2, sl st to the ring. Fasten off.

Tip: as you work the pattern into the ring, scoot the stitches closer together so all the stitches can fit around the ring.

- Tie the second color around the center ring and knot to finish. Don't tie the knot too tight! You still want to be able to see the center. Wrap the yarn again around the body for a bit more thickness. Tie another knot at the top of the butterfly, then trim the antennae to finish.

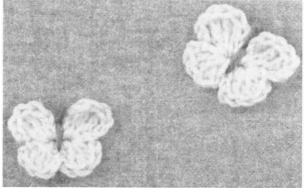

6. Single Crochet.

Materials List
- Crochet hook of choice
- Yarn of choice

How to Single Crochet:
- Insert your hook into center of your next working chain. Grab yarn (known as a yarn over) and draw through the chain stitch and up onto the hook so that you have two loops on your hook.

- Using your hook, grab yarn and draw it through both loops on your hook, leaving just one loop on your hook. You've made one single crochet stitch.

- Repeat steps 1 and 2 as many times as your pattern calls for.

7. Hand Chain Sashay Scarf.

Materials

- 150 yards of Lily Sugar 'N Cream Cotton Twists Yarn by Yarnspirations in Overcast or any worsted weight (4) cotton yarn (1 ball makes 3 dishcloths)
- Boye Crochet Hook Size J 6.00 mm
- Yarn needle
- Scissors

Abbreviations

- sc = single crochet
- tr = triple crochet
- ch = chain
- st = stitch

Notes

- *Finished size is 7"x 7"*

- *To make this dishcloths in different sizes use a multiple of 2 then add 1 to whatever length you have chosen.*

The Textured Dishcloth Pattern Steps
- Foundation Row: ch 25
- Row 1: Starting in second ch from hook sc, sc in every ch across, turn. (24)
- Row 2: Ch 1, in first st sc, tr in next st, *sc in next st, tr in next st, repeat from * across ending with 1 sc in each of the last 2 sts, turn. (24)
- Row 3: Ch 1, in first st sc, sc in every st across, turn. (24)
- Row 4: Repeat Row 2 (24)
- Row 5: Repeat Row 3 (24)
- Row 6-14 Repeat Rows 2 & 3 alternately (24)
- Fasten off and weave in loose ends throughout

8. Dishcloth Crochet Pattern.

Supplies:
- *2 strands of category 4 (medium/worsted) yarn held together, OR 1 strand category 6 (bulky) yarn (1-2 skeins, depending on desired length)
- *Size K (6.50 mm) crochet hook
- *Optional: button, yarn needle

If you're using Category 4 yarn, you need either to get 2 skeins of yarn, or divide your skein into two balls. This makes it easier to work while holding two strands of yarn together.

Crochet Chain Necklace Pattern

- Row 1: Chain until all your yarn is gone. Sl st into 1st ch. Fasten off.

Of course you can use more or less yarn, depending on how long you want it. For a lighter or shorter necklace, you may not use the whole skein. For a thicker more scarf-like necklace, you may want to use the whole skein plus a little more. Experiment a little. After all my yarn is gone, I slip stitch to my first chain and fasten off, then fold the long ring in half, in half again, in half again, etc. until it is the right size for a necklace. Play around with it until you find what you like best.

At this point you can either just wear it as is, like this more summery crochet necklace. . .

Or you can add a little button tab to add a little interest. This also keeps the lengths of chain together so they don't get unwieldy or tied up in a knot.

Button Tab Pattern

Stitch explanation: sl in flo = slip stitch in front loops only. This means you work the sl st in only the loop that is closest to you instead of both loops.

- Ch 16.
- Row 1: Sl st in flo of 1st ch from hook and in each ch across.
- Rows 2 - 5: (Ch 1, turn. Work sl st in flo of each sl st across) repeated 4 times. Fasten off, leaving a 10" tail for sewing. Wrap tab around necklace

strands and stitch ends together with a yarn needle. Sew on a button in the middle of the tab if desired.

Made in United States
North Haven, CT
14 April 2025

67949560R10019